BRITAIN IN OLD PHOTOGRAPHS

TAUNTON REVISITED

NICK CHIPCHASE

SUTTON PUBLISHING LIMITED

Sutton Publishing Limited
Phoenix Mill · Thrupp · Stroud
Gloucestershire · GL5 2BU

First published 1998

Reprinted in 2002

Copyright © Nick Chipchase, 1998

British Library Cataloguing in Publication Data
A catalogue record for this book is available from the
British Library.

ISBN 0-7509-1960-4

Typeset in 10/12 Perpetua.
Typesetting and origination by
Sutton Publishing Limited.
Printed in Great Britain by
J.H. Haynes & Co. Ltd, Sparkford.

YE OLDE TUDOR HOUSE, 15 Fore St., TAUNTON.
Containing Showrooms and Galleries replete with interesting examples of
Old World Furniture; China, &c., for sale at strictly commercial prices.
F. G. HALLIDAY, (1909) Ltd., Antique Dealers.
Ye Odds & Ye Ends, Taunton, Minehead, Eton, Banbury and Porlock.
Specialities: Week-end Cottages furnished throughout. Collections formed and augmented.

Ye Olde Tudor House, 15 Fore Street, Taunton.

CONTENTS

	Introduction	5
1	Streets & Buildings	7
2	Religion & Education	17
3	Commerce	25
4	Transport	43
5	Sport & Leisure	67
6	People & Events	75
7	Public Houses & Hotels	95
8	The Villages	103
	Acknowledgements	126

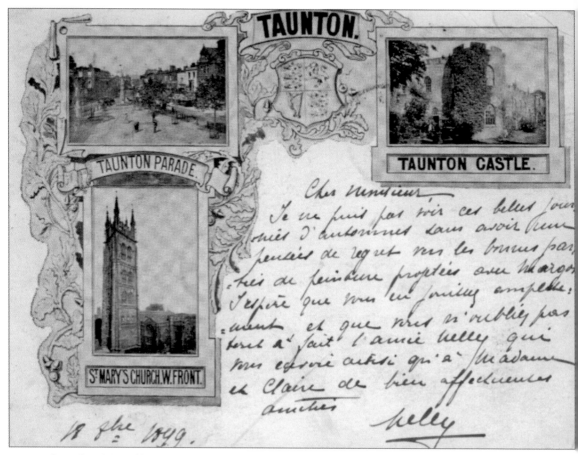

The earliest known Taunton postcard, postmarked October 1899.

INTRODUCTION

After a period of five years, I am now happy to present a companion volume to my other two books in this series, *Taunton In Old Photographs*, and *Around Taunton In Old Photographs*. This book offers for view another two hundred photographs, most of which have not been published before. The first modern book of historic Taunton views was produced by George Frederick Talbot, who semi-retired from Hinton's the gunsmith in 1959. His book *Taunton Yesterday and Today* appeared in the mid-1970s. Such is the pace of change in the town that many of the 1970s views are now hardly recognizable. Indeed, since the publication of my last book the town centre has been completely redeveloped. Whether we like it or not, Taunton and the surrounding area seem destined to expand rapidly over the next twenty years. It is a far cry from the quiet street scenes of fifty or more years ago.

This third selection has enabled me to publish some of the rarer photographs in the collection. In the first book I felt obliged to cover the main streets and public buildings, but this selection includes views of some of the more obscure back streets and I have also been able to feature the early days of the motor industry in the town. In the final chapter in the book I have included some of the more unusual village photographs. The quiet and self-contained village life I knew as a child is now almost gone forever. Progress does not necessarily mean improvement, and I hope that some of the photographs in this book will remind readers of this. Taunton has a unique character – it would be nice to believe this can be preserved in the hectic decades to come.

Nick Chipchase, 1998

Taunton's official coat-of-arms. This design of a cherub's head and Saxon crown was granted by the College of Arms in 1934. The previous version depicted the Imperial crown, which can only be borne by the monarch's special permission. The winged cherub's head above a crown has been traced back to a hand seal of 1685, bearing the motto 'Defendamus'.

CHAPTER ONE

STREETS & BUILDINGS

A maintenance platform for the carbon arc lamp, Mary Street, c. 1890. The Dove Inn can be seen on the left while the tower on the right is part of Mary Street School, built in 1886. The Dove Inn and most of the left-hand side of the street were demolished in 1960 during road widening. (Art Portrait Co., Cardiff)

Jubilee Street, Rowbarton, *c.* 1904. In those days the street consisted of thirty-two houses, and residents included a joiner, an undertaker, a dressmaker and a bootmaker. This is one of a series of anonymous coloured postcards of the Rowbarton area.

William Street, Rowbarton, *c.* 1902. The Greenway Estate was established by Thomas Penny (1827–1906), on land bought at Greenway Farm in 1885. Together with his son (also Thomas), he was responsible for much of the development at Rowbarton where the streets were named after his sons and grandsons. (Brice, Taunton)

Gladstone Street, Rowbarton, *c.* 1905. This was also part of Penny's development. Gladstone, Rosebery, Asquith and Harcourt streets were all named after Liberal statesmen. The buildings on the left are part of the Somerset Steam Laundry. (E.E. Cox, Taunton)

Gloucester Street, *c.* 1905. This is one of those quiet backwaters rarely seen on postcards.

The old stone arch bridge over the River Tone, *c.* 1890. This was replaced in 1894 by the present structure. This overhead view shows that the bridge was relatively narrow, and with the opening of the railway station in 1842 and subsequent development at Rowbarton it became less of a practical proposition. On the right is Bridge House, now obscured by the Dellers Wharf development. On the left is the Tone Bridge Iron Foundry, which evolved into Allen's motor business around the turn of the century. The damage to the photograph was caused by sellotape – a product not recommended for archival purposes.

Eastbourne Road and Terrace, *c*. 1905. This is another of those elusive back street views produced as postcards but hardly a viable proposition in terms of sales. This view contains over seventy children – the current record holder for any Taunton street scene! (W.A. Crockett)

Motor cars are lined up alongside the Parade, Fore Street, *c*. 1925. The large building on the left is the Victoria Rooms, built as the new market in 1821 and demolished in 1963. The building housed the meat and vegetable market until 1929 and a British Restaurant during the Second World War.

The approach to the Bridge, *c.* 1918. W. & A. Chapman's department store is on the left with St James's Street to the right. It is very quiet in terms of traffic, with just one motor car and one horse and cart.

Lyngford Farm, *c.* 1904. This former rural area of Taunton has now been extensively developed. The farmhouse still exists off Lyngford Road, albeit in a different form. It was owned by the Tavender family in the early 1900s.

Fore Street, *c.* 1865. This early street view was published on a *carte de visite* by Webber & Blizard of 52 East Street. John Blizard, a former schoolmaster, entered into partnership with John Webber, a commercial photographer, in 1864. The partnership lasted fewer than ten years and Webber was trading alone by 1872.

John Moore's forge at 23 East Reach, *c.* 1906. John Moore is the bearded man in the centre. The original photograph was copied by George Talbot and is now presumed to have been lost.

Bridge Street, *c.* 1922. This view appears to post-date the removal of the tramlines in 1921, although the overhead cables still seem to be in place. The narrow exit from Wood Street was later widened by the demolition of the Labour Exchange. (Valentine)

Kingston Road, *c.* 1900. This view shows St Andrew's Working Men's Clubhouse before its removal to the other side of the street (see page 74). The club opened in 1885 with a beef and plum pudding supper for 150 people.

Park Street, *c.* 1925. Photographs of the street from this direction are rare. St Paul's House, on the corner of Park Street and Tower Street, was purchased by Taunton Corporation in 1929. The building stood on the site of the Carmelite Monastery of St Paul, and served as the Convent of Perpetual Adoration from 1867.

North Street, *c.* 1903. Double-decker trams were replaced by single-deckers in 1905. A passing loop can be seen on the single-track tram line; ten such loops were incorporated in the system. The terminus was situated at the bottom of East Reach. (Brice)

East Street and the London Hotel, *c.* 1905. The horse bus was introduced by the hotel proprietor in 1903. Also shown here are a GWR delivery cart and Arthur Steeven's furniture emporium. On the right is Hook's Teapot, indicating the type of business conducted there. Other similar rebus trademarks were Baker's harp (musicians) and Fisher's giant kettle (ironmongers). (Chapman, Dawlish)

Blake Street, *c.* 1905. This scene has changed little in the intervening ninety years though now, like most side streets, it is usually well stocked with motor cars. (Crockett)

CHAPTER TWO

RELIGION & EDUCATION

Fullands School, c. 1905. The building is quite old, possibly dating back to the late 1600s. In about 1820 the house, which had long been untenanted, was converted into a lunatic asylum. In 1840 a classical school was established and it was here that General Gordon received his early education. Fullands School closed in 1888 and in more recent years the building was used by Kings College. The house and surrounding area have now been redeveloped. (Abraham)

Aerial view of Taunton School, *c*. 1930. The school opened in 1847 as the Independent College in a terrace of houses on the Wellington Road. The present site was acquired in 1870 and the school became known as Taunton School in 1899. (Aerofilms)

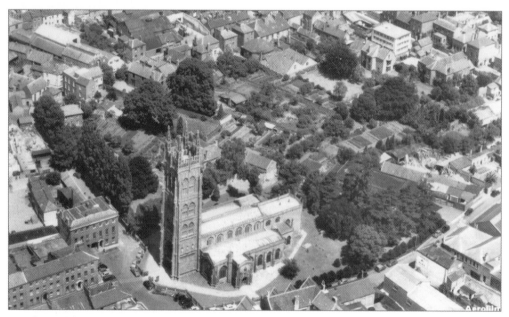

Aerial view of St Mary's church, *c*. 1930. The church tower is the most prominent building in Taunton. The development of Hammet Street in 1788 opened up the fine view that we have of the tower today. Like St James's Church, St Mary's tower was rebuilt in the last century (1858–62), a faithful copy of the original. (Aerofilms)

Pauls Meeting House, *c.* 1904. This building was erected in 1797 on the site of the old meeting house built in 1662 and is the oldest Nonconformist place of worship in Taunton. Various groups used the meeting house, including a boys' club, mothers' meetings, Christian Endeavour, choir practice, Band of Hope and Sunday School. (Abraham)

St Mary's church, *c.* 1910. This rather unusual view of the church was taken in Magdalen Street near the corner of Canon Street. (Boalch's Series)

North Town School Standard II, *c.* 1914–16. Miss Miller is seated in the centre with twins Stan and Wilf Ridgeway, born 19 March 1907.

The girls of Group 9, St James's National School for Boys and Girls, *c.* 1914.

A geography class in progress, Taunton Girls School, *c.* 1925. The school was situated at the vicarage at St Mary's church but had moved to Burnham-on-Sea by 1930. This is a view from the series originally featured in *Taunton in Old Photographs*. (Buchanan & Co.)

Bishop Fox's School, Staplegrove Road, *c.* 1918. This view, part of a series of at least twelve postcards, shows the main hall. A number of local schools, including the Convent, commissioned sets of postcards at around this time. They give an interesting view of school life in the early twentieth century. The school relocated to Kingston Road in 1940. (Buchanan)

Interior view of the Temple Wesleyan Church, Upper High Street, *c.* 1902. The church was built in 1808 on land purchased by James Lackington, a native of Wellington.

North Street Congregational Chapel, *c.* 1905. The chapel and part of the school premises date from 1842 when they were erected by the members of the Congregational body who had separated from Paul's Meeting. In 1884 the dwelling house that blocked the frontage was removed. (Abraham)

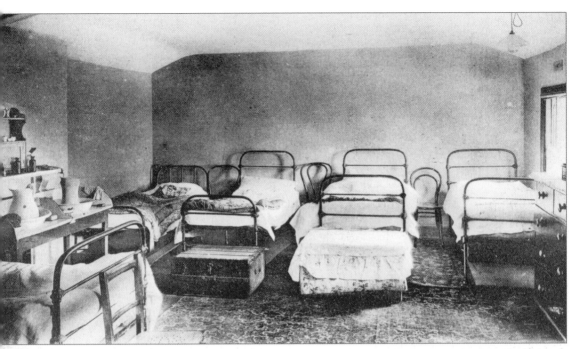

A rather spartan-looking dormitory at Weirfield School, *c*. 1918. No doubt today there would be posters all over the walls and much more expression of individuality. Note the washstand with jug and basin sets to the left. (Buchanan)

The gymnasium at Weirfield School, *c*. 1918. There's nothing too sophisticated here, a piano for exercises to music, a beam and some ropes, but the girls did have the benefit of a nice warm stove. (Buchanan)

The kindergarten, Weirfield School, *c.* 1918. Despite the caption on this postcard, I have a feeling that this is actually a view of the gymnasium looking the other way. It was not unusual for girls' schools to run mixed classes for infants. In this view the children are sitting rigidly to attention, their hands behind their backs. (Buchanan)

Queens College swimming pool, *c.* 1910. The pool was opened by Lady Hart in 1908 and is still in use today. (W.A. Crockett)

CHAPTER THREE

COMMERCE

Parade Market, with Hammet Street and the tower of St Mary's, c. 1884. In this year Henry Massingham gave an electric lighting display at Taunton. The Parade was electrically lit on a permanent basis by Massingham in 1886. Taunton was the first town in the south-west to adopt such a system.

Pickfords' shop, 3 North Parade, Station Road, *c.* 1905. Mr Tribe stands in the doorway. Pickfords' services included foreign and general carriage, removals and warehousing. Ocean passages could also be booked.

Hole and Bryant's garage at 30 East Reach, *c.* 1925. The site was redeveloped in the 1960s to form Rex Brothers Motors Ltd.

North Town Stores, *c.* 1915. This popular shop was situated at 19 Bridge Street.

Bruford's shop, 150 East Reach, *c.* 1906. In 1904 Brufords was listed as a toy shop. This view from a few years later suggests that the stock has become a little more diversified. Although no longer a shop, this distinctive building remains much the same today. (E.E. Cox)

F. Gardiner's shoeshop at 29 High Street, *c.* 1905. This super postcard is typical of the cards commissioned by businesses in the early 1900s. The poster advises potential customers that they can order made-to-measure shoes from 14*s* 6*d* for gents and 10*s* 6*d* for ladies. A trade directory tells us there were thirty-three shoemakers in Taunton in 1902.

Tom Serle was another local shoemaker who ran his business from his home at 1 (later 3) Ivy Cottages, Kingston Road. Tom is pictured here with his wife Polly in about 1903.

Cecil Dawkins in the doorway of his shop at 3 Carlton Terrace, Station Road, *c.* 1906. Mr Dawkins, lately removed (i.e. the proprietor was already an established local trader) from Collard & Collard in North Street, lived at 5 Malvern Terrace. There is a nice selection of phonographs on display.

Pool Wall factory, *c.* 1905. In the early part of the nineteenth century there was a silk works on this site, but by the mid-1860s linen collars were being produced here by Young & Co. In 1882 the mills were occupied by the Taunton Manufacturing Co., which were engaged in the manufacture of shirts and collars. The factory closed in 1958 and was demolished. (Crockett, Taunton)

The staff of Pool Wall, photographed on 28 September 1899. This is one of a series of full-plate photographs showing all aspects of work in the factory. The original album containing twenty or so photographs still survives in private hands. (Crockett, Taunton)

Pool Wall factory, 1937. This is the shirt room decorated for the coronation of George VI in 1937.

The Parade, *c.* 1888. This was the commercial centre of Taunton, now extensively redeveloped. In front of the Kinglake Memorial (erected 1867) can be seen one of Massingham's original electric light installations.

Tolman's, East Reach, 1902. Another coronation view, but this time for Edward VII. J. Tolman, later Tolman & Son, was well known as a baker and corn merchant. Faded writing on top of the building still testifies to that fact.

F. Cullen and Co.'s Taunton Scale Works, c. 1912. This business was situated in Upper High Street and disappeared when the street was widened. The youngster on the left is Ted Cullen.

Marshalsea's garage, Fore Street, *c.* 1912. This postcard view is dated 1912 and possibly shows the opening of the garage. The company previously operated as carriage builders at 55 East Street. The business was opened by the Marshalsea brothers from Ilminster. (M. Cooper)

Marshalsea's garage, *c.* 1912. By the early 1920s, Marshalsea's had opened a motor body building factory and showrooms on the site of a former rollerskating rink at Wellington Road. The works were gutted by fire in 1923. (M. Cooper)

S. Luckes Works, St James Street, *c.* 1946. The workers pictured here include Harry Riley, Jack Mills, Joff Summers, Bill Winter, Bob Hooper, Jim Pearce, Ted Broom and Geoff Radford.

Harry Riley, blacksmith, at work in S. Luckes Works, *c.* 1946.

Thomas Biffin's chemist's shop at 56 North Street, *c.* 1880. Thomas Biffin had the business between 1878 and 1884, and the building had housed a chemist's shop since the 1830s when it was occupied by Hitchcock & Son. The last occupant was Boots Cash Chemist Ltd. The Kinglake Memorial is in the centre of the street.

Sidney Wilfred Shepherd, wine and spirit merchants, at 58 High Street, *c.* 1927. Part of the premises was formerly occupied by the Bell Inn. In the 1950s the Old Bell Inn Yard was home to S.H. Shattock, motor engineer, Taunton Dye Works and the workshop of Law & Son, house furnishers. Starkey Knight and Ford originated as G. Knight of Bridgwater, becoming Starkey Knight and Co. around 1888. In 1895 the company amalgamated with Ford of Tiverton Brewery. The company owned Northgate Brewery in Bridgwater and the Taunton Brewery, together with a number of public houses and hotels in the area. Starkey Knight and Ford Ltd were acquired by Whitbread Flowers Ltd in 1962.

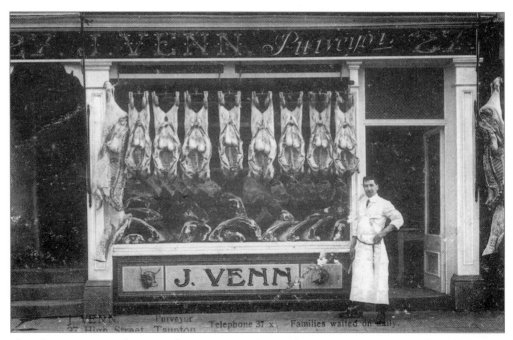

This advertising postcard was sent by Mr J. Venn of 27 High Street in 1916. Mr Venn himself, knife in hand, stands beside this fine display of disembowelled carcases. Hygiene laws or perhaps good taste would preclude such a spectacle today. (W.A. Crockett)

Eades' posting establishment, *c.* 1902. D. Eades & Son were also furniture removers with premises at 31 East Reach. This is one of those classic anonymous little postcards that occur by the thousands in dealers' stocks. Only the notice about Bridgwater and the characteristic trees prompted me to buy and research the photograph. There is definitely a Taunton 'feel' about this view.

Taunton Market, c. 1902. The market was held on the Parade on Wednesdays and Saturdays. Auntie Gin, who sent this card to Olive, wrote that 'this is where we get all the cheap things on Saturday'. (Senior & Co., Bristol)

Taunton Market, pictured at its current site off Priory Bridge Road, 1953. The car LYA 736, an 1172cc Ford, was registered to C.R. Richards of Rexhill Farm, Bathpool. Motor taxation records are a useful aid to dating and research of old photographs; they are kept at the County Record Office. The market site was opened by the Mayor of Taunton in December 1929.

Penny's timber yard off Wood Street, *c.* 1900. The yard was established by Thomas Penny in 1876. Although most of the area is now a car park, it is likely to be redeveloped to include a link road in the future.

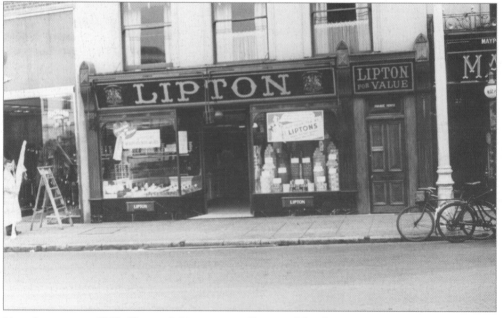

Lipton's grocery, *c.* 1930. Thomas J. Lipton personally opened his shop at Fore Street in 1890. This is a much later view of the shop with the Maypole Dairy Co. next door.

The Model Dairy, Staplegrove Road, *c.* 1902. The business was owned by Samuel J. Wright, who also opened the Rowbarton butter factory in about 1900. This business subsequently became Somerwest until it closed in the 1980s and the premises were demolished.

Priory Farm dairy, *c.* 1937. The decorations are probably for the coronation of George VI. The business was established in 1896. The two vehicles are a Singer Goods and a Jowett Goods (CYA 123) which Mr W.J. Howe acquired at the end of 1936.

Interior view of the Newton Electrical Engineering Works Ltd, Rowbarton, *c.* 1905. Newtons manufactured dynamos, Mawdsleys patent motors, transformers, etc. The company was established in 1891 and the factory closed in 1934.

W.H. Westlake & Son, 65–66 High Street, *c.* 1907. The premises were situated next to the Saracen's Head Inn. Westlake's specialities were school suits, sport suits and complete outfits.

Hatcher & Sons Ltd, High Street, *c.* 1905. The business was started by William Hatcher at Marnhall in Dorset and subsequently moved to Taunton, taking over premises formerly occupied by a linen drapery established by Matthew Colman next to the County Hotel in 1788. The business thrived and moved to the High Street. In 1898 Hatcher's was registered as a limited company. Today, Hatcher's is a member of Associated Stores Ltd, the largest independent voluntary non-food buying group in the UK. (M. Cooper)

This interior view of the Taunton Electricity Works in St James Street in 1899 shows Bellis and Morcom steam engines coupled to BTH alternators.

Staff at the Electricity Works, *c*. 1900. The St James Street works were established in 1889 on the site of the Old Priory Collar Works. At the turn of the century the works served 510 connected consumers as well as operating the public lighting system. In 1901 the works also supplied power to the tramway system. In real terms, the cost of electricity was much greater in 1900 than it is today. The works closed in 1937 and were eventually demolished. This view also shows the switchboard and Ferranti rectifier.

CHAPTER FOUR

TRANSPORT

Chapman's stores and steam delivery wagon, c. 1905. By 1920 the firm had acquired Leyland motor delivery vans. The premises at the bottom of North Street are now owned by Debenhams Ltd. William and Arthur Chapman Ltd occupied the site from 1864 to 1972.

W.J. King's brand new Sentinel steam wagon DG 4T. The vehicle, a four-wheel tipper, was registered by King's on 20 April 1926. The designed speed for the vehicle was 12 mph but it could reach 50 mph downhill when out of gear. On one such speedy occasion, Ted Pike, a local driver, ran into the back of a horse and cart belonging to Derby the corn merchant and driven by Mr Sedgebeer. The unfortunate animal was catapulted on top of the hedge while the driver was buried in the corn. Steam vehicles could also be a fire risk when passing the numerous thatched cottages in rural Somerset. In 1942 King's had four Sentinel DG 6s and one S4. Several of these old vehicles have been restored. See page 123 for further details. (Sentinel)

Another of W.J. King's vehicles, *c.* 1945. This is a heavy steam road roller with chain steering.

Horse vans waiting outside the Somerset Sanitary Steam Laundry's Rowbarton premises, *c.* 1910. Customers' washing was fetched and delivered within a 6 mile radius of Taunton.

Pony and Ralli Car outside Hetherton Park, *c.* 1904. The Ralli Car was a direct descendant of the dogcart and took its name from a member of the Ashtead Park family. Ralli Cars were built in quite large numbers around the turn of the century. Their main distinguishing feature is the side panels, which were designed in such a way that they curved over the wheels to form splashboards. The methods of suspension varied considerably.

Allen's Motor Works, *c.* 1904. Charles Allen acquired the works at the Tone Bridge Iron and Brass Foundry in the 1870s. This early postcard view shows the original frontage, behind the centre of which a large gas engine drove the workshop machinery.

Allen's Motor Works, *c.* 1910. This is a later view of the frontage after the gas engine had been resited and the central section remodelled. The wording on the wall has now been amended to read Motor Repair Works. William Allen and his wife lived in the flat above the works.

William Allen, pictured outside his works, *c.* 1906. The other gentleman is possibly Mr Mynors, the works foreman. The *Taunton Courier* office can be seen in the background. The car has no number plate, so must date from 1900 or 1901.

Arthur C. Allen in a Beeston Humber, a 30 hp motor car, *c.* 1908.

Allen's workshop, *c.* 1906. The company built its own range of cars using de Dion engines. The badge on the radiator stated CCC, probably standing for Chassis Construction Co. It would seem that the cars were not particularly successful as only seven CCC cars, with various body types, were registered in Somerset between 1906 and 1911. The first such vehicle, a 20 hp, 19 cwt 'dog cart body' car, was registered in November 1906. In August 1907 C.E. Esdaile of Cothelstone acquired a 19½ cwt double phaeton, and other later types included a landaulette, wyndham and tonneau.

Allen's premises, *c.* 1905. At this time, Allen's also taught people to drive. One pupil, a former groom, always pulled on the steering wheel and shouted 'whoa' when he wanted to stop.

Allen's Daimler of *c.* 1900 towing a wreck (probably an 1899–1901 Benz or Renault) on the trolley used for breakdowns, pictured outside the works, *c.* 1906. The nightwatchman's doorway is on the right. Arthur Allen is in the white coat on the left. (H. Stainer)

A vehicle in need of repairs at Allen's Motor Works, *c.* 1910. 'Dumb irons' formed part of the steering mechanism and were prone to damage. The timing cover is at the front of the engine.

This Chevrolet 22 hp car, pictured at Allen's Motor Works, was registered to James Brook of Golden Farm, Tolland, in 1922. The Chevrolet was introduced in 1912 and imported in crates by Allen's in the early 1920s. In 1927 the car became America's best-selling marque, producing over a million cars in a year for the first time.

Allen's Chevrolet show, 1928. The main vehicle on view in the top photograph is the Chevrolet Curtis single horsebox (complete with dummy horse). In the lower photograph, the van with the hand belonged to W. & A. Chapman. In December 1929 Allen's organized a convoy of Chevrolet commercial vehicles which toured the district in an effort to popularize the make.

Another photograph of Allen's Chevrolet show, 1928. The two vehicles in the foreground are a Star (right) and an Armstrong-Siddeley (left). The house inside the showroom was later demolished.

Charabancs requisitioned for army service, 1914. The vehicles were modified by having truck bodies fitted and left Taunton in September 1914. The vehicle in the centre is a 3 ton 11 cwt Karrier, formerly owned by Staddon & Sons of Minehead. (M. Cooper)

Edwards' Motors, *c.* 1905. Edwards' Motor and Cycle Agents opened in Corporation Street in April 1903. Willie Pearse Edwards is standing behind the cars. C. Webber is sitting in Y465, a 6 hp two-seater, nicely styled in green with black mouldings. This car was sold in 1906 to W.F. Wittingham, a Taunton wine and spirit merchant who became mayor in 1911. The other car (Y532) is an 8–10 hp Vinot owned by Mr Edwards himself.

Harry Ferguson Ltd tractors on a Luckes' Bedford delivery lorry, 1956. These tractors were first introduced by S. Luckes in October 1956. They boasted a host of new features and appeared in Ferguson grey and rich metallic bronze.

Edwards' trade stand, 1924. The lady in the centre is Hilda Beach, wife of Eddie Beach, the proprietor of Beach's Motor Works. E. Robson, the cricketer, died in 1924 and a benefit match was arranged for his family. Edwards donated a prize motorcycle for anyone guessing correctly the attendance at the Somerset vs South Africa match. In 1951 W.P. Edwards (Motors) Ltd were trading as motor cycle agents at 58 East Street. These premises were later acquired by Wadham Stringer (Taunton) Ltd, distributors for Austin, Wolseley and MG. W.P. Edwards (Motors) Ltd moved their business to the service station in Station Road next to the Classic Cinema.

These two photographs show Stone's garage, Staplegrove Road, *c.* 1906. Y519 is a 16–20 hp Beeston Humber 4 cylinder 18 cwt side-entrance touring car. The other vehicle is either a Darracq or an Argyll. A disastrous fire occurred at the garage in December 1907 (see *Taunton in Old Photographs*, page 112).

Beach's Motor Works in St James Street, *c.* 1911. In this year, Mr Beach was advertising his business as Beach's Aeroplane Works. The machine here appears to be powered by a version of the Gnome rotary engine, introduced in 1908, which revolutionized the development of powered flight.

Lorries of the Australian Siege Battery parked in Portman Street, *c.* 1917. Many of the soldiers were billeted with the local residents.

Two advertising postcards for Beach's garage, *c.* 1905. Note the telephone number, 28Y. There were fifty-four Taunton subscribers to the National Telephone Company in 1902 but Beach's was not at that time included. The car pictured above is a Daimler. The car shown below is almost certainly a 1901/2 10 hp Mors, with an East Sussex registration. Note the rear entry to the back seat, chain drive and the skid chains on the rear tyres. These prevented skidding and were used all the year round, not just in winter.

Interior of Beach's Pioneer Motor Works, *c.* 1915. In the centre is Y2203, a Humber car with a touring body, owned by George Barling of the Langport Arms Hotel. During the 1920s Beach's also had a garage at Greenway Road which was bought by Edwards & Sons in 1927.

James Beach in a French-manufactured Aries motor car, pictured in Greenway Road, *c.* 1905. This machine was shaft-driven with a double rear axle. (M. Cooper)

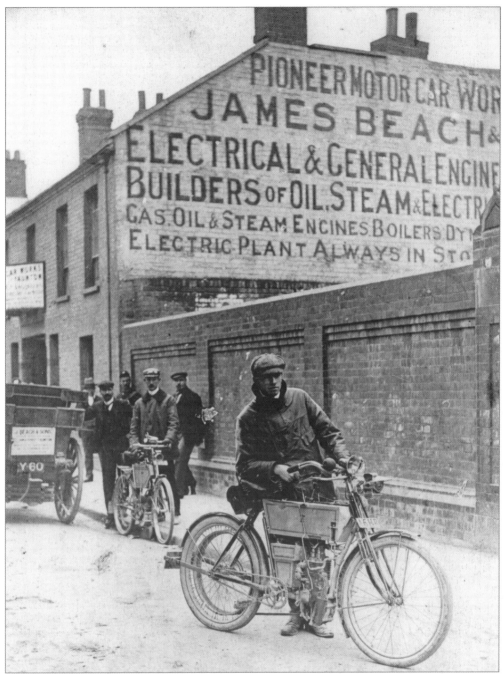

Beach's Pioneer Motor Car Works, 1904. Beach's were great self-publicists, as the writing on the wall in St James Street clearly shows. The year 1904 was the first year of compulsory motor registration. Y60 is a 6 hp Motor Manufacturing Co. (MMC) 19 cwt tonneau body vehicle. MMC was based in Coventry and cars were built between 1897 and 1908. This car was finished in black and red. The gentleman in the foreground is Mr Bramley-Moore, who was due to take part in the Edge Cup on his 2¼ hp Hulbert-Bromley motorcycle, a machine built in Putney in 1903. Sadly, in the event the crankcase plug fell out, causing the engine to seize through lack of oil. (H. Stainer)

Eddie Beach on his penny-farthing cycle in Portman Street.

Motorcycles outside Clarke's Hotel, *c.* 1912. Three of the machines can be identified by their registration numbers: Y1002 is a 3½ hp Rex, Y997 a 2¼ hp twin Enfield and Y1036 a 3½ hp Phelon & Moore.

A delivery cart belonging to the Taunton Co-operative and Industrial Society, *c*. 1902. The side of the cart bears the Society's Magdalene Street address. The Co-operative Society subsequently expanded the site and opened the town's first major supermarket in East Street. Long considered an architectural eyesore, the store's frontage was remodelled in the mid-1990s.

Pony and governess cart, *c*. 1910. This happy couple was photographed in the Lyng area. The postcard was published by Mitchell of Creech St Michael (possibly John Mitchell, carrier of Bull Street). Most of Mitchell's photographs appear to originate in the Creech–Lyng area.

Taunton station, *c.* 1950. The first passenger train arrived at Taunton on 1 July 1842. Originally Taunton was on the Bristol & Exeter Railway but the B&ER was amalgamated with the GWR in 1876. The station was extensively remodelled in the 1930s. The massive stone wall that formed the eastern side of the engine shed is still a major feature of Station Road, just before the railway bridge.

The 14.13 train to Minehead waiting at West Down Bay, Taunton station, 1959. The train is headed by engine no. 5543, a 2–6–2T 4575 Class locomotive. The other engine is no. 5798, a 0–6–0PT 57XX Class.

No. 3027 *Worcester*, a 4–2–2 GWR locomotive at Taunton station, *c.* 1905. (E. Poteau)

No. 4985 *Allesley Hall* at Taunton, *c.* 1962. This 4–6–0 locomotive was allocated to Taunton in 1959.

A GWR express train taking on water at Creech troughs, *c.* 1910. The 560 yd long troughs were opened in 1902 and enabled locomotives to re-supply on non-stop runs between Paddington and Exeter.

Holt tractor on Station Approach, *c.* 1916. There are a number of postcard views of Holt tractors moving through Taunton, apparently heading towards the station. Holt tractors were petrol-driven American agricultural machines modified to haul large-calibre guns on the Western Front during the First World War. Eventually it was decided to mount the guns on the caterpillar tracks and further experiments resulted in the development of the tank. (M. Cooper)

This 4 hp BSA was registered to Mr Cox on 31 May 1915. This postcard was produced by the studio of photographer E.E. Cox.

Edwin Smith's Carriage Works in Haydon Road, *c.* 1910. The premises were formerly owned by L. Whateley. Smith's were coach-builders specializing in the manufacture of wagonettes, phaetons, dog carts, rustic and business carts. (M. Cooper)

A 20 hp Model T Ford in Fore Street, *c.* 1920. Tudor House behind was occupied by Halliday's antique shop from 1909 to 1946.

The Parade and Market House arcades, *c.* 1927. The vehicle turning left into Corporation Street is a 10½ hp Wolseley, registered in 1926. The other vehicle is a 1922 27½ hp Chevrolet. Despite the lack of road users by today's standards there is a policeman directing traffic in the centre of the roundabout. The Market House arcades were removed in 1930.

CHAPTER FIVE

SPORT & LEISURE

Eddie Mullins outside his hairdressing shop in Station Road. He is seated on his motorcycle, an Ariel Colt 250cc, before the London to Land's End Run at Easter 1934.

Members of the Taunton and West Somerset Gliding Club, help to assemble Captain Lowe-Wylde's two-seater glider at the gliding demonstration at Musgrove Field in July 1934. Included are David Clements, C.M.B. Kite, R.H. Penny, G. Lock and C. Allen.

Captain Lowe-Wylde in flight in the Gliding Club's new one-seater machine, 1934.

Captain Lowe-Wylde's machine gave flights to the public at the airfield in 1934. The aircraft was towed by a motor car until it became airborne.

Captain Lowe-Wylde (BGA) and Mr Barker, Chairman of Taunton and West Somerset Gliding Club, 1934. The Club's new machine was presented by the President, Lieutenant-Colonel Hamilton Gault MP. It was later put on display at C. Allen & Sons Motor Works.

Taunton Post Office Football Club, 1908/9. Back row, left to right: F.G. Berry, S. Woocott, F.H. Knight, S.T. Andrews, G. Kekevich, F.A. Hurford, F.G. Allen. Middle row: C. Phillips, P. Hancock, F. Hull, T. Chambers, F. Beel. Front row: E. Tucker, P. Stone.

Taunton Red Cross Football Club, 1917.

Taunton Harriers Athletic Club, 1906/7. The Club was formed in 1882. It met at its headquarters at the King Alfred Temperance Hotel. Members ran on Tuesdays and played football on Thursdays. Back row, left to right: H. Hole, H. Quick, F. Lillycrap, F. Stone, H. Dominey, G. Hughes, O. Planck, J. Duckworth, F. Panting, J. Holman. Middle row: W. Bodley, W. Vickery, A. Bullock, R. Chown, J. Coles, A.H. Trenchard, H.J. Coles, W. Nash, H. Bond, C. Taylor. Front row: J. Burge, E. Burgess, J. Standfast, E.G. Boulting, L. Birkbeck, H.J. Van Trump, H. Scott, W.A. Arnold, W.A. Male.

Bishops Lydeard football team, 1928/9. The club was formed in 1912. The team pictured here includes F. Durman, J. Sully, J.H. Fox, F. Ames, Revd F.C. Fitch, L. Saunders, R.A. Colman, W.J. Shallis, H. Holcombe, H. Davey, E. Musgrove, R. Stephenson, H. Blackmore, F.C. Hillier and F. Sully. (E.E. Cox)

Long Run Farm and Hunt, *c.* 1908. The local packs at this time included Taunton Vale Foxhounds, Taunton Vale Harriers, West Somerset Foxhounds, Quantock Staghounds, and Devon and Somerset Staghounds, as well as several beagle and otter hound packs.

Taunton Vale Harriers at Fosgrove, *c.* 1904. The Harriers had kennels at Blackbrook and met on Monday and Thursday. (Crockett)

Taunton YMCA 1st Eleven, 1905/6. Back row, left to right: S. Trebble, H. Taylor, J.F. Goodland, E.S. Luff, B. House, J. Jeffery, S.A. Spiller. Front row: P.R. Chanin, F.J. Nuttall, E.W. Slade (Captain), H.H. Hook, P.A. Clode, G.A. Male.

Taunton Bicycle Club, pictured outside the Municipal Buildings, 1900. The club was formed in 1877 and was based at the George Hotel. There were a hundred members with the benefits of a club badge and optional uniform. This is the earliest known dated photograph of a motor car in Taunton, although one probably passed through the town on a journey from John O'Groats to Land's End in 1897.

These two photographs show the removal of the St Andrew's Working Men's Clubhouse from one side of Kingston Road to the other in August 1905.

CHAPTER SIX

PEOPLE & EVENTS

Monsieur Selmet, the French aviator, at Taunton, 29 May 1912. M. Selmet landed near the Quaker burial ground at Halcon Corner, en route from South Wales to Chard during the Daily Mail *Air Race. The correspondent has marked the postcard to show where he was standing.*

M. Selmet's machine on the ground at Taunton, 1912. M. Selmet was officially welcomed by the Mayor of Taunton, Ald. W.F. Whittingham. Despite the very cold weather, M. Selmet delighted the crowd by taking off again and circling the ground a number of times before landing. There was much local interest in the flights. The local (*Somerset County*) *Gazette* reported that 'Shepherds neglected their sheep and stonebreakers sat with their hammers gazing intently at the sky.'

The People's Theatre Company, 1906. The tall figure at the back, H. Dalton, sent this card to a nurse at Cheddon Road Hospital with the note 'Pardon my liberty – hope to see you once more.' In 1907 Mr Hayes and his company returned for their third season and opened the People's Theatre Company at Jarvis Field (now the site of the market).

The staff of the Van Heusen collar factory assembled in Prince's Street, *c.* 1940. Mr Jones of New Zealand is in the centre at the front. Also included are Mr Hartley (managing director), Mr Wilkins (cutter) and Mr Dunlop (manager).

Van Heusen's No. 5 Platoon of the Home Guard, pictured outside the factory, *c.* 1940. The Home Guard's orders for one particular week were: Monday, On duty all night; Tuesday 7 pm, Lecture on the Chinese Gestapo; Wednesday 2 pm, Parade, evening free; Thursday 7 pm, Lecture on how to be a soldier; Friday, Lecture on parts of a rifle; Saturday, Skittles match between nos 1 and 2 Sections versus nos 4 and 5 Sections; and Sunday, All morning parade.

Taunton Carnival, shortly after its revival in 1922. The fire engine is a Dennis registered by Taunton Fire Brigade in February 1924.

Pool Wall carnival float, c. 1928. Second from right at the back is Beatrice Perry and next to her Bessie Osman. The man on the right in the white coat is Frank Bourne, the shirtroom foreman.

Taunton Carnival, *c.* 1925. At this time the procession took place during the daytime. Taunton Carnival is now one of the south-west's premier carnival events. It is held annually during an evening in the autumn.

Taunton Carnival, 1907. The mixed bathing float won first prize in the comic section. (E.E. Cox)

Taunton Carnival, Saturday 1 October 1927. The Volga Boatmen entry was assembled by the staff of the *Somerset County Gazette* and won Best Feature prize. The same float also won the Championship Prize at Chard. Right to left on the boat: G. Stuckey, H. Chalk, R. Reader, B. Winsborrow, G. Bond, A. Cornish, C. Tucker, J. Doble, C. Nettell, W. Fry, W. Best, S. Ware, B. Gill, W. Stone, T. Dominey, J. Thorne, W. Millard.

Taunton Carnival, 1921. To mark the end of tramcar service in the town the body of the last Taunton tramcar was hauled through the town by traction engine. The placard on the roof of the car is a parody of the hit song of the period, 'Yes, we have no bananas!' The tramway system had opened in Taunton in August 1901. Single-deckers replaced the six original double-deckers during 1905 when the tracks were relaid on granite setts. The service ceased on 28 May 1921. This view was taken from the end of Belvedere Road.

Sanger's Circus fire, July 1920. This is the only known photograph of the tragic big top fire at Jarvis Field in which six people died.

Floods in Station Road, 1960. The Plough Inn is on the left.

Floods at the junction of St James Street and North Street, 1960. W.T. Maynard & Co. Ltd's popular café is at 18–19 North Street.

This aerial view shows the extent of the flooding along Station Road in 1960. At the top the market and cricket ground are submerged while Flook House stands as an island in the lower centre. Flook House was occupied by Miss Sibley and her Ladies Collegiate School in 1902. In 1907 during the widening of Station Road the large boundary well was demolished together with the George Inn, now the site of the Classic Cinema. Taunton Corporation acquired the house in 1946 and this now houses the Registry Office. A new swimming pool for the town was built in the grounds together with a local government headquarters (see also page 101).

A Starkey Knight and Ford delivery van braving the floods near the railway bridge, 1960.

A big freeze took place in January 1963. Allen's staff are pictured here playing football on the ice on the River Tone. The hole near the bridge was made by an RSPCA officer for the benefit of the river birds.

Bertram Mills' Circus elephant, *c.* 1953. This view of Victoria Park was taken from Priory Bridge Road; the Taunton School bell tower is on the left.

The High Sheriff's Trumpeters, pictured outside the Castle Hotel, 1933. (Photochrome Co.)

Lord Robert Baden-Powell, 1919. He is pictured at the Vivary Park County Rally following the opening of a new Scout headquarters in North Street, a gift of Sir Jesse Boot.

Princess Helena Victoria and the Marquis of Bath greet the officer commanding the guard of honour, Captain J.W. Harper, during her official visit in 1934. This photograph was taken in Corporation Street.

Taunton Historical Pageant, 26–30 June 1928. The pageant took place under the mastership of Major M.F. Cely Trevilian. Its six episodes endeavoured to show the story of our country from an angle that history books often failed to portray, illuminating the feelings, aspirations, hopes and fears of the ordinary people caught up in the national events depicted.

Flook House staff, c. 1915. In the centre is Lucy Mockridge (later Rugg) of Bishops Hull. The Sibley family sold the house and grounds to Taunton Corporation in 1946.

Pool Wall factory outing, 1949. These are girls from the offices, shirt laundry, collar laundry and stockroom.

The funeral of Abraham Yard at Albemarle Baptist Chapel, 1909. A fifty-year-old employee of Mr T.S. Penny, the timber merchant, Mr Yard was fatally injured when he fell between the shafts of his timber wagon at Wrantage. (M. Cooper)

Mr Hunt, dairyman, delivering milk by bicycle. As yet this business has not been traced in the trade directories, so information would be welcome.

Prams in Vivary Park, 1904. The bandstand and ornamental gates were added in 1895. The park celebrated its centenary in 1994. Behind the bandstand is the keep of Jellalabad Barracks, formerly the home of the Somerset Light Infantry. The design of the towers, which were completed in 1881, is attributed to the army's Divisional Surveyor, Thomas Berry. (Tuck)

Smith's bookshop, pictured after it collapsed on the night of 7 December 1959. The exposed side of Smith's had been buttressed after the demolition of Boots the chemists to make way for the new £250,000 Lloyds Bank building. Christmas stock valued at more than £1,000 was buried in the rubble but fortunately nobody was in the building at the time. On-site safety standards were certainly less stringent in the 1950s: there is not a helmet to be seen.

A youthful Duke of Edinburgh, possibly on a visit in 1952 when he officially opened Taunton Green. I also seem to remember a visit in about 1960 when we schoolchildren were marched up the town to line the route of the procession.

W.H. Stone, the proprietor of Stone's Garage, pictured in his Singer landaulette, *c.* 1906.

Vivary Park, June 1897. The marquee had been erected for the occasion of the Queen's Diamond Jubilee celebrations. The umbrellas suggest inclement weather but, in fact, it was a very hot day. Victorian ladies had no great love of the sun and the ruddy complexion it afforded. Note the little lad in the sailor suit, a fashionable dress for boys at the time. The marquee was used to provide a public lunch. Other aspects of the celebrations included a dinner for 700 over-60s in the Corn Exchange and Municipal Hall. Five thousand Sunday School children received a Jubilee medal and a free tea. The Market House was decorated with flags and banners and the message 'God Save the Queen'. The Victoria Rooms and Parade received similar attention (see *Taunton in Old Photographs*, pages 92 and 93).

Trull School nativity play in the church at Trull, *c.* 1953. The author is the very angelic type second from the left. At the risk of embarrassing my former schoolmates, I can also name Raymond Lock, Susan Bobbet, June Govier, Ann Redwood, Marguerite Woolley and Janet Hawkeswell.

The First World War tank at French Weir, *c.* 1925. The tank arrived in 1919 to mark the raising of war savings by Taunton. It was sold for scrap at the start of the Second World War.

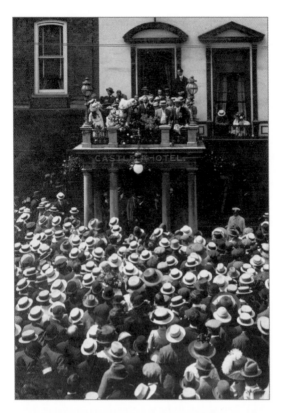

Lt-Col. Boles' declaration of poll at the Castle Hotel, *c.* 1911. Lieutenant-Colonel Sir Dennis Fortescue Boles of Watts House, Bishops Lydeard, was MP for West Somerset from 1911 to 1918. He continued in office as MP for the Taunton Division until 1922. (H.H. Hole)

Staff at Tone Vale Mental Hospital, *c.* 1950. The hospital was founded at Bishops Lydeard in 1897. It has now closed and the site is being redeveloped.

CHAPTER SEVEN

PUBLIC HOUSES & HOTELS

The Half Moon Hotel, North Street, c. 1904. Owned at that time by Hanbury and Cotching, the hotel was acquired by Starkey, Knight and Ford in 1923 and their galloping horse trademark can still be seen on the building which now houses a shoe shop.

Gardeners Arms, Plais Street, *c.* 1904. The building bears the date 1897 and was rebuilt on the site of Plais Street House on Priorswood Road.

The Prince Albert public house (previously the Bird in Hand), 19 Mary Street in 1927. In 1960, when Mary Street was widened, Selwood's Antiques moved into the premises from their building across the road, which was then demolished.

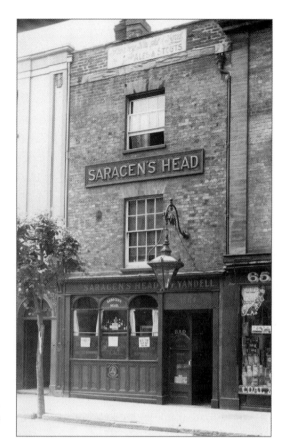

The Saracen's Head, 64 High Street, 1927. The pollarded trees were a feature of Taunton's streets in the early 1900s (see also pages 36 and 41). Many have now disappeared although some still remain in Corporation Street.

The Somerset Temperance Hotel, 80 Station Road, c. 1930. At this time it was run by Harold Moggridge. The temperance movement had its heyday in the early years of the century. There were five Temperance Hotels in Taunton in 1904, including the now well-known Ashton Hotel in Station Road.

The Fleur de Lys on Hamilton Road, *c.* 1935. This was a temporary name adopted by the Rose Inn from 1932 to 1938, apparently for licensing reasons.

The Old Angel Hotel in Corporation Street, *c.* 1910. This pub was recorded as early as 1688 and was renamed the Sportsman's Inn in 1956. The building has now been demolished. (M. Cooper)

The Waggon and Horses Inn at 122 East Reach, 1912. The previous Waggon and Horses Inn was gutted by fire in 1867.

The Green Dragon Inn on the High Street, *c.* 1950. At this time the premises were owned by Arnold and Hancock Ltd, an amalgamation of S.W. Arnold & Sons of Rowbarton Brewery and William Hancock of Wiveliscombe which took place in 1929.

The Crown and Saracen's Head Hotels, High Street, *c.* 1967. Much of this area has been redeveloped and part of the new area of shops has been named Crown Walk.

A painting showing the Royal Marine Inn and Silver Street, *c.* 1900. Also included is the Convent building in the distance. The pub and adjoining buildings were demolished when the road was realigned and the surrounding area redeveloped to form the site for Sainsbury's supermarket.

Demolition of the George Inn, 1907. The inn stood on the corner of Staplegrove Road and Station Road. In 1913 the Lyceum Cinema (later the Classic) was built on the site. (H. Montague Cooper)

A charabanc outing pictured outside the Crown and Sceptre Inn, *c.* 1915. The original premises were thatched and the present structure dates to 1899.

The Winchester Arms, *c.* 1905. The Taunton livestock market was originally held in the area between the Winchester Arms and Clarke's Hotel, now the Castle. Sheep pens can be seen in the foreground. In the late 1920s the area became the town's first designated car park. (Harvey Barton)

The Victoria Inn, East Reach, *c.* 1912. This view shows the building before renovation.

CHAPTER EIGHT

THE VILLAGES

Athelney signal-box, c. 1905. Athelney station opened on 1 October 1853 on the Yeovil line from Taunton to Castle Carey via Langport. There was also a connection from Athelney via Durston to Bridgwater. The line closed in June 1964.

Athelney, *c.* 1905. This view was taken from the level-crossing. Behind the lady is the now chimneyless cider house of Bill Becks. The sheds on the left were originally built for the storage and drying of withies for use in basket-making and traditional crafts. (David Edwards Stores)

Floods in Athelney, 1929. The lady in the boots is Kathleen Boobyer and the photograph was taken close to the breach in the embankment at Curload at a point known as the Sheilings.

Repairing the river embankment at Athelney, 1929. During the first two weeks of December much of the Taunton area was hit by severe weather. Vivary Park and parts of the town were flooded. At Curload efforts to contain the River Tone finally failed and the river burst its banks during the early hours of the morning. Much of the area had to be evacuated. Sixty families were made homeless at Burrowbridge and in the worst affected area, the parish of Stoke St Gregory, there were 120 homeless families. A county relief fund was set up to aid the homeless.

Trull village, *c.* 1845. The view is from an oil painting originally in private hands but now the property of the parish. There is a farmhouse on the left and Wadham Cottages to the right. The author's family home is behind the horse and cart.

Pitminster, *c.* 1904. This view shows two postmen with Mr James Buckland to the left. Pitminster post office was destroyed by fire in 1955.

Amberd Lane, Staplehay, *c.* 1910. This lane, although still in the countryside, looked a lot more rural in 1910 than it does now.

Billy Bicknell's workshop and house, Staplehay, *c.* 1910. The Crown Inn is on the extreme left. Billy Bicknell was the local joiner and coffin-maker; a garage now stands on this site. (J.J. Marsh)

Bishop's Hull, photographed from the church tower across the roof of the old vicarage, *c.* 1905. The thatched Old Inn can be seen in the centre.

Bishop's Hull schoolchildren, *c.* 1924. Ken Rugg is second from the right in the middle row. The old school at Bishop's Hull opened on 11 July 1893 in Gipsy Lane. Attendance rose to a peak of 351 children in 1958. New school buildings were completed near the church in 1978. (Vickery Bros)

Galmington village, *c.* 1906. This view is hardly recognizable today as all the cottages on the right and the terrace on the left (The Rank) have been demolished. The photograph was taken outside the Galmington Inn, now the Shepherd's Rest. One of the walls of The Rank remains as a boundary alongside Shepherd's Hay. A companion view to this photograph, looking in the opposite direction, appeared in *Around Taunton in Old Photographs*. Galmington was originally a small hamlet in the parish of Bishops Hull. It is now the focus of a large residential development in the newly extended area of Comeytrowe. The road in the photograph originally ended at Galmington stream through which access could be gained to the continuation of Hoveland Lane, the former boundary of the Borough of Taunton. Much of Hoveland Lane was replaced by Galmington Road about forty years ago.

Church Hill, Bradford on Tone, *c.* 1905. The first two cottages still exist but the thatched cottages beyond were demolished in about 1910 and the village hall built on the site. The photograph below shows the same view after the construction of the hall. The foundation stone was laid by the Right Revd Bishop Wilkinson on 22 November 1911.

North Curry Club annual walk, 1908. The club had 100 members. It was finally wound up in 1912 after the passing of the Insurance Act, which required all village clubs to become approved Friendly Societies.

Staff of the Hatch Park Red Cross Hospital, *c.* 1915. The hospital at Hatch Park opened in May 1915. Its six wards contained twenty-six beds for injured servicemen. The matron was the Hon. Mrs Gore Langton (centre). The hospital was further extended by the use of Mynd House and Oakfield.

Thornfalcon School, *c.* 1906. Thornfalcon was a small village and parish with a population of 173 in 1901. The school closed in 1962 and the children were transferred to Creech St Michael.

Higher Street, Curry Mallet, *c.* 1905. This photograph was taken by local photographer, J.F. Bridel, whose postcards are often marked with the initials JFB.

Baby Show, Curry Mallet, 1912. This is the only photograph I have seen of a baby show. One wonders if there were prizes for the bonniest baby. Doubtless the judges would have to be very tactful. The lady under the window is Sarah Keates, with her baby May.

The postmaster Mr Harold Turner and his dog stand outside North Curry post office, *c.* 1942. (H.C. Turner)

Curry Mallet Jazz Band, *c.* 1905. Mid-centre is Bill Keates and at the back centre Percy Mico. The dog presumably took no part in the musical activities.

Curry Mallet Cup Final outing, 1924. The fans are off to Stoke St Gregory to see the match. The Bell Inn is in the background.

Stoke St Gregory Baptist Sunday School outing, *c.* 1910. One can almost sense the excitement in this fine cavalcade. There are lots of best bonnets and dresses and the horses are well turned out with their gleaming brasses.

Lyng village, *c.* 1908. The parish had a population of 280 in 1901 and included the famous Isle of Athelney.

Lyng schoolhouse, *c.* 1908. This public elementary school was erected in 1875 for sixty children. It is now a private house.

Walter Cozens, baker of Ruishton, *c.* 1905. At this time Ruishton had a population of around 500. Like most small villages it was well served by local tradesmen. Listed in the 1904 directory are a baker, a butcher, bookmaker, laundress, two shopkeepers, two carpenters, two market gardeners and an innkeeper.

The coronation celebrations for George V at Creech St Michael in 1911. This photograph was taken outside the New Inn. (Mitchell)

Creech St Michael, *c.* 1920. This photograph was taken from the church tower and shows the canal and railway bridges. Much of the landscape has now been filled by modern houses.

Creech schoolhouse and school, *c*. 1907. The school was built in 1873 and closed in 1983. It catered for 149 children in 1898, and numbers rose steadily to a peak of over 250 in the 1970s. More than 100 evacuee children came to the school during the Second World War. In April 1962 eleven children and a teacher were transferred here from Thornfalcon School which had closed.

An unusual postcard of Creech St Michael, *c*. 1905. The view is only identifiable by the church in the background, and it may portray the annual Village Bazaar. All of the ladies are wearing bonnets or hats and the customary hot weather parasol is much in evidence.

Funeral procession at Bishops Lydeard, *c.* 1910. The cortège is in St Mary Street (now the High Street).

Sand Hill, Bishops Lydeard, *c.* 1905. The house was built in 1720, forming part of the Lethbridge Estate until 1913. During the Second World War it was used as an American Army hospital. The postcard was sent to Miss R. Board from 'Dad', who evidently considered himself to have a little medical knowledge: 'Mrs Prateley died this morning – tumour on the brain. Saunders, the postman, fainted down in the field below our house – something wrong in his stomach.'

The almshouses, Bishops Lydeard, *c.* 1910. The police station, the first building on the left, was given up in 1974, after many years. The sign 'Purveyor' on the shop beyond indicates the premises of O.A. Keirle, formerly occupied by Lickfold, butcher, whose business was established in 1825.

Bishops Lydeard school, *c.* 1910. The cottages to the left of Piffen Lane were demolished to make way for a launderette and branch library. The school was built in 1872 and modernized in 1977.

This postcard of the post office at Bishops Lydeard was posted in 1910 but 'was taken some time ago'. The little girls are called Molly and Nora.

Bishops Lydeard Working Men's Institute was erected in about 1906. The timber building housed a billiard club and the village library run by schoolmaster Mr Tipper. It was removed to make way for the new village hall which was completed in 1939.

Watts Lane, Bishops Lydeard, *c.* 1906. Watts Lodge is on the left with the gates to Watts House (now Cedar Falls). Watts Cottage, on the right, was originally a tied cottage for Watts House. It has been extensively altered since 1906 and now has a front-facing gable.

David Hanks outside Hank's shop, Bishops Lydeard, *c.* 1932. At the turn of the century, Walter Hanks ran the horse-bus 'Punctuality' from Bishops Lydeard to Taunton. By the early 1920s a motor bus was in use and this operated until 1933. The fare in 1902 was 6*d* single and 10*d* return.

Foden steam wagons in W.J. King's yard at Bishops Lydeard, *c.* 1930. The drivers, from left to right, are Bert Cavil, Lewis Newton, R. Howard, Fred Cross, J. Sully and B. Hitchcock. The man in the cap is the yard foreman, Tom Hitchcock. The Fodens were taken out of use in 1933 but many of King's vehicles survived in various states of repair to be auctioned and restored. In 1971 Foden YA7962 and Sentinel S4 Tipper YD8148 were sold but the most memorable auction was held in the yard in 1988. The vehicle shown second from the right, a 1925 Foden three-way tipper (MP9405), fetched £5,500. Other registrations sold in 1988 were TU219 (Foden), TU3113, TU1215, LG544, LG2347 and LG4815. One vehicle had a tree growing through its chassis which had to be cut down before the buyer could remove it. The yard was redeveloped for housing.

Norton Fitzwarren charabanc outing, *c.* 1920. The vehicle on the left belonged to Frank Northcott of Albemarle Road and was a 30 hp Garford of 2 tons 1 cwt. Note the varied collection of hats and caps.

West Monkton Auxiliary Fire Brigade, *c.* 1942. They are pictured outside Proctor's Farm, where the appliance was stored. The brigade was formed in 1941 and met at the Gardener's Arms once a week. They practised on Saturdays.

Kingston St Mary, *c.* 1908. The car, a 9 hp MMC, belonged to the photographer Henry Montague Cooper. The building on the right housed the stores and bakery. The thatched cottages beyond were demolished in about 1920.

Lydeard St Lawrence, *c.* 1905. The shop in the foreground belonged to Alfred Pullen, grocer, draper and baker. It is now the post office. Chapel Cottage on the left remains but it has been substantially altered. The parish had a population of 390 in 1901.

ACKNOWLEDGEMENTS

The author would like to thank the following people for their help in the compilation of this book.

Mr J.B. Villis • Phyllis Eason • John Upham • Mrs Yard • Mrs Bourner • Miss I. Crossman
the late Bill Board • Mrs J. Colmer • Grace Poole • Mr W. Stephens, late of Allens Ltd
Pat and Fred Gamlin • Mr M. Spender • Mr Peter Parrish • Miss Beel • Brian Wilkinson
Mrs J. Hinton • Ted Pike • Taunton Camera Centre • Joan Harris • Wendy Trollope
the late Ken Rugg • Mrs Van Heusen • Mrs K. Hill • David Bromwich at the Local
Studies Library • Jim Boulton for his help in identifying car marques

If readers can supply additional information or lend original photographs for copying, I
hope they will contact me via Sutton Publishing.

BRITAIN IN OLD PHOTOGRAPHS

Aberdeen

Acton

Amersham

Ashbourne

Around Bakewell

Balham & Tooting

Barnes, Mortlake & Sheen

Barnet & the Hadleys

Barnet Past & Present

Bath

Beaconsfield

Bedfordshire at War

Bedworth

Belfast

Beverley

Bexley

Bideford

Bilston

Bishop's Stortford & Sawbridgeworth

Bishopstone & Seaford II

Blackburn

Bletchley

Bloxwich

Braintree & Bocking at Work

Brentwood

Bridgwater & the River Parrett

Bridlington

Bristol

Brixton & Norwood

Buckingham & District

Bury

Bushbury

Camberwell, Peckham & Dulwich

Cambridge

Cannock Yesterday & Today

Canterbury Cathedral

Canterbury Revisited

Around Carlisle

Castle Combe to Malmesbury

Chadwell Heath

Cheadle

Chelmsford

Cheltenham in the 1950s

Cheltenham Races

Chesham Yesterday & Today

Around Chichester

Chiswick & Brentford

Chorley & District

Around Cirencester

Clacton-on-Sea

Around Clitheroe

Colchester 1940–70

Coventry at War

Cowes & East Cowes

Around Crawley

Cromer

Croydon

Crystal Palace, Penge & Anerley

Darlington at Work & Play

Darlington II

Dawlish & Teignmouth

Around Devizes

East Devon at War

Dorchester

Dorking Revisited

Dumfries

Dundee at Work

Durham: Cathedral City

Durham People

Durham at Work

Ealing, Hanwell, Perivale & Greenford

Ealing & Northfields

The Changing East End

Around East Grinstead

East Ham

Around Eastbourne

Elgin

Eltham

Ely

Enfield

Esher

Exmouth & Budleigh Salterton

Farnborough II

Fleetwood

Folkestone II

Folkestone III

The Forest of Dean Revisited

Frome

Fulham

Galashiels

Around Gillingham

Gloucestershire at Work

North Gloucestershire at War

South Gloucestershire at War

Goudhurst to Tenterden

Grantham

Great Yarmouth II

Greenwich

Greenwich & Woolwich

Hackney II

Hackney, Homerton & Dalston

From Haldon to Mid-Dartmoor

Hammersmith & Shepherd's Bush

Hampstead to Primrose Hill

Around Harrogate

Harrow & Pinner

Hastings & St Leonards

Hayes & West Drayton

Around Haywards Heath

Around Helston

Around Henley-on-Thames

Herefordshire

Around Highworth

Hitchin

Holderness

Hong Kong

Huddersfield II

Huddersfield III

Ilford to Hainault

Ilfracombe

Ipswich Revisited

Islington

Jersey III

Kendal Revisited

Kensington & Chelsea

East Kent at War

Keswick & the Central Lakes

Kingston

Kirkby & District

Kirkby & District II

Kirkby Lonsdale

Knowle & Dorridge

The Lake Counties at Work

Lambeth, Kennington & Clapham

Lancashire

The Lancashire Coast

Lancashire Railways

East Lancashire at War

Lancing & Sompting

Leeds in the News

Around Leek

East of Leicester

Leicester at Work

Leicestershire People

Letchworth

Lewisham & Deptford III

Lincoln

Lincoln Cathedral

The Lincolnshire Coast

The Lincolnshire Wolds

Liverpool

Llandudno

Around Lochaber

Theatrical London

Loughborough

Lowestoft

Luton

Lye & Wollescote

Lympne Airfield

Lytham St Annes

Around Maidenhead

Manchester

Manchester Road & Rail

Mansfield

Margate II
Marlborough II
Marylebone & Paddington
The Melton Mowbray Album
The History of the Melton
  Mowbray Pork Pie
Merton, Morden & Mitcham
Middlesbrough
Around Mildenhall
Milton Keynes
Minehead

The Nadder Valley
Newark
The Norfolk Broads
Norfolk at Work
North Walsham & District
Northallerton
Around Norwich
Nottingham Yesterday
  & Today

Oldham
Ormskirk & District
Otley & District
Oxford Yesterday & Today
Oxfordshire at Play
Oxfordshire at School
Oxfordshire Yesterday & Today

Penwith
Penzance & Newlyn
Around Pershore
Peterborough
Around Plymouth
Poole
Portslade

Prestwich
Putney & Roehampton

Redditch & the Needle
  District
Richmond
Rickmansworth
The River Soar
Around Rotherham
Royal Norfolk Regiment
Rugby & District II
Ruislip
Around Rutland
Around Ryde

Saffron Walden
St Albans
St Andrews
Salford
Salisbury II
Sandhurst & Crowthorne
Sandown & Shanklin
Around Seaton & Sidmouth
Sedgley & District
Sedgley & District II
Sheffield
Sherwood Forest
Shoreham-by-Sea
Lost Shrewsbury
Southampton
Southend-on-Sea
Southwark, Bermondsey &
  Rotherhithe
Southwark, Bermondsey &
  Rotherhithe II
Southwell
Stafford

Around Staveley
Stepney, Bethnal Green &
  Poplar
The History of Stilton
  Cheese
Stockport
Stoke Newington, Stamford
  Hill & Upper Clapton
Stourbridge, Wollaston &
  Amblecote
Stowmarket
Stratford, West Ham & the
  Royal Docks
Streatham II
Stretford
Stroud & the Five Valleys
Stroud & the Five Valleys II
Suffolk
Suffolk at Work II
Sunderland
Sutton
A Swindon Album
Swindon III

Around Tamworth
Along the Thames
Around Thirsk
Tipton
Tipton II
Around Tonbridge
Torquay
Around Truro
Twickenham, Hampton &
  Teddington

Uley, Dursley & Cam
Upminster & Hornchurch

The Upper Fal
Uxbridge 1950–1970

Ventnor

Wallingford
Walsall Revisited
Waltham Abbey
Walton-on-Thames &
  Weybridge
Wandsworth at War
Around Warwick
Weardale
Weardale II
Wednesbury
Wembley & Kingsbury
West Wight
Weymouth & Portland
Around Wheatley
Around Whetstone,
  Totteridge & Finchley
Whitchurch to Market
  Drayton
Wigton & the Solway
  Plain
Willesden
Wimbledon
Around Windsor
Wisbech
Witham & District
The Witney District
Wokingham
The Women's Land Army
Woolwich
Worcestershire at Work
Wordsworth's Lakeland
Wotton-under-Edge to
  Chipping Sodbury

SUTTON'S PHOTOGRAPHIC HISTORY OF TRANSPORT

Jaguar
Jensen & Jensen-Healey
Lotus
Morgan
Rolls-Royce

TVR
Vauxhall
Suffolk Transport
Manchester Road & Rail
Manchester Ship Canal

Black Country Railways
Cheshire Railways
Derbyshire Railways
Devon Railways
Lancashire Railways

Shropshire Railways
Warwickshire Railways
Worcestershire Railways
Steam around Reading
Steam around Salisbury